Grandma Stays
in the Heart Forever

A Children's Book about

Illness, Dying and Death

1st Edition, 2020

Idea and Text:
© Daniela Landsberg, 2019

Editor:
Daniela Landsberg
c/o Familie Moltrecht
Zum Thelenkreuz 22
53859 Niederkassel-Mondorf

Title and Coverdesign:
Dr. Rolf Peter Hampel-Landsberg, MD
Daniela Landsberg

Illustrated by:
Dr. Rolf Peter Hampel-Landsberg, MD
Daniela Landsberg

Printing/Publishing: BoD- Books on Demand, Norderstedt

ISBN: 9783751960830

Bibliographic information from the German National
Library:
The German National Library lists this publication in the
German National Bibliography; detailed bibliographical
data are available on the Internet at http://dnb.d-nb.de.

Many thanks to Bianka and Ty Stumpf from Sanford, North Carolina, USA. With your painstaking help, both in the corrections and in the advice and suggestions, the story of little Emma could appear in English.

In the waiting room

"Tick tock, tick tock, tick tock." Emma sits in the hospital waiting area looking at the big, round clock with its red second hand. She has been waiting here for more than half an hour. Actually, they had wanted to visit Grandma like every Saturday as before, but Grandma has been in the hospital for a long time. Emma's mom has said that Grandma is not feeling well at the moment and needs a lot of rest.

An elderly gentleman with a hat enters the waiting area. "Hello, young lady," he greets Emma warmly. "Hello, sir," Emma replies in a friendly way, too. The older gentleman sits down opposite to Emma. "Alone here?" he asks her. Emma shakes her head, "No, I'm still too small for that. I'm only five." Emma lifts her right hand up and spreads her fingers apart. "Look, I'm that old!" she announces to the older

1

gentleman. "Well, then you are really too small to be alone here," he says. "Yes, I would say so," Emma says. Emma looks at the clock again, then she shares, "My grandma has cancer." "Cancer," repeated the older gentleman, "ah, that's not good."

"No, my mom said you can die from that," replies Emma. "That's unfortunately right," says the older gentleman. "Cancer is a bad guy, a really bad guy," Emma says angry. The older gentleman looks at the floor thoughtfully. Emma first thinks to herself but then asks the older gentleman, "Why are you here? Does your grandma also have cancer?" He shakes his head and answers quietly, "No, not my grandma...my wife has cancer." Then Emma continues, "And did your mom put you here now, too?" Emma looks at the older man with big eyes. He laughs but then gets serious again, "No, little girl. My parents are long dead. They died before you were born." Emma raises her eyebrows. "Then you are

2

an orphan," she says with a start. The older gentleman has to laugh again. "Yes, that's the way to say that. You are pretty smart for such a little girl," he notes. "My mom and dad always say I'm pretty smart," then Emma hesitates for a moment, "but they also say that sometimes I talk a lot and am fidgety. That's why Daddy sometimes calls me Whirlwind," she adds. "But are not all little girls your age like you?" asks the older gentleman. Emma muses, "I do not know. The kids in my Kindergarten class are sometimes a bit different. But that does not matter. I still play with them," Emma laughs. "Do you have any children?" Emma wants to know. "No, unfortunately, my wife and I did not have any children," the older gentleman replies. "That's probably sad because then you're all alone and nobody plays with you," Emma says. She then offers, "If you want, we can play together. You can swing on my swing in the garden or slip on my slide. You just have to take care with your big

3

legs so you do not hurt yourself." The older gentleman smiles again broadly.

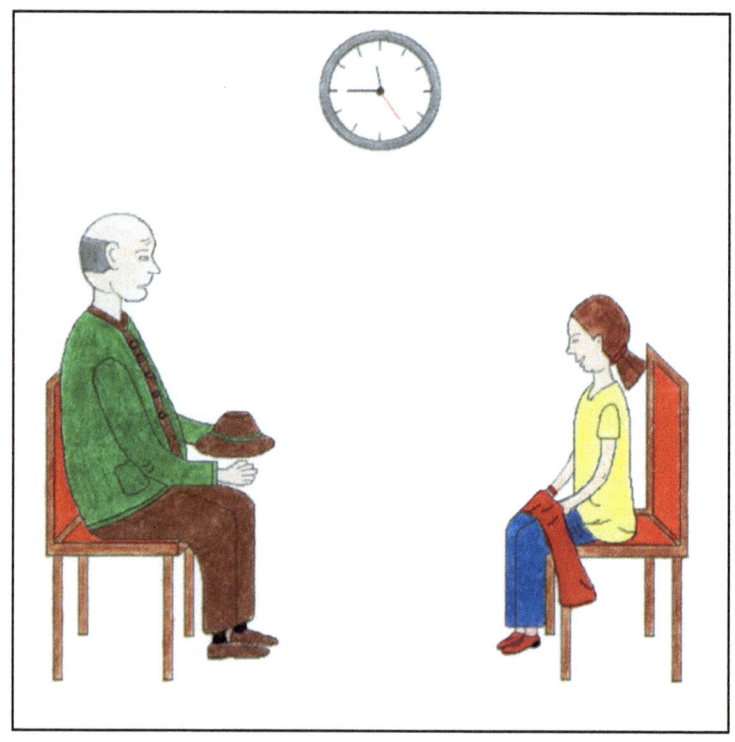

At that moment, Emma's mother comes in the door, greets the older gentleman, and then turns to Emma, "Are you coming, little one? You can go to Grandma." Emma hops from her chair, "Oh, great! Is grandma better?" she wants to know from her mother. Her mother shakes her head, "No, Emma, unfortunately not." Emma asks, "She is not getting well anymore, is she?" Her mother shakes her head again, "No, Emma, she will not get better." Emma looks at the older gentleman, then asks, "What's your name?" The older gentleman averts his eyes from Emma's mother and answers, "My name is Alois."

"Alois," Emma repeats, "that's a funny name you have there." Emma wrinkles her nose. Alois laughs, "This is not a funny name. That's an old name," he tries to explain to Emma. "Well, then you have a funny old name." Emma hesitates for a moment and then adds, "But you're still nice."

"Thanks," Alois replies, "I'll gladly give back the compliment." Emma's eyebrows contract with thought. Then she asks, "What's a compliment?" Alois smiles and replies patiently, "That's when you say something nice to someone."

"Then I'll pay Grandma a compliment, too. Maybe she will be happy about that," Emma declares. Alois nods, "Definitely, Emma. Most people are happy about compliments." Emma adds, "Then you also have to compliment your wife, so she's happy too, right?"

"Yes, I do", says Alois. Emma smiles, "That's nice."

Emma goes to the door, turns around again, and beckons, "Take care, Alois." Alois waves back and answers, "You too, little Emma." Sighing, Alois stays behind. "A little grandchild, that would have pleased Erna," he says quietly to himself. "Erna..."

On the hospital corridor

Excited Emma runs across the hall. She is very happy to see her grandmother again. She was not allowed to visit her grandmother the last time because she was too weak. Emma thinks, "If Grandma has been too weak for a visit the last three times, but she is even worse today, why can I see Grandma today?" Just as she asks the question to her mother, she begins, "Emma, if we go to Grandma's room now, Grandma will look a little different than you're used to." Emma's mom thinks about how she can prepare her daughter for the sight. Was it really the right decision to take Emma to the hospital? Should not she remember her grandma as she knew her? Emma notices her mother's hesitation. Carefully, Emma asks, "Did Grandma cut her hair?" Emma's mother shakes her head. "Maybe she has new glasses?" Emma continues. Once again, Emma's mother shakes her head. Emma thinks hard. Then she remembers, "Papa has seen a documentary because there was also a woman cancer. She did not have any hair left." Emma pauses, then continues, "Does Grandma not have any hair anymore?"

"But Emma, Grandma still has her hair. The woman in the documentary got chemo, and that's why her hair fell out."

"Did grandma not get chemo…chemotherapy?" Emma asks. The mother shakes her head, "No, Emma, Grandma has a very bad cancer. You cannot cure it. Besides, Grandma…" Emma's mother hesitates, "Grandma is a bit older. She does not want to have chemotherapy." Emma puts her little hands on her hips and scolds, "Grandma is not old!"

"Ok, not that old. However, she does not want to do chemo because she does not want to suffer. In addition, the cancer is already well advanced," Emma's mother tries to explain. Emma beams, "But that's good. If the cancer is already well advanced, it means that he soon will be completely gone." The mother thinks, "No, Emma, that's not what it means." "Yeah, how is that meant then?" Emma asks impatiently. "Emma, if the cancer is already well advanced, it does not mean that it goes away..." "But?" Emma interrupts her mother. "It just means that the cancer has become so much that you cannot get it away anymore. You cannot heal it anymore," Emma's mother tries to explain to her daughter. "But you just said that Grandma does not want to have chemotherapy because Grandma is too old! Then you can still cure Grandma. She just has to do the chemotherapy and then the cancer goes away," Emma notes firmly. The mother sighs, "Emma, the chemotherapy...this is a very powerful drug that would run through Grandma's body. Grandma feels so weak that she does not want to." The mother hesitates, but then continues, "In addition, the cancer, as I have already explained

9

to you, is very advanced, that the doctors assume that Grandma would not become well again. And then comes Grandma's age. So, all that matters, which is why Grandma decided against chemotherapy. Can you understand that?" Emma's mother looks at her daughter sadly. How she would like to spare her daughter all this. Again, the thought of whether it was the right decision to take Emma to the hospital with her. For days she thought about it. Imagined how Emma would react at the sight of her grandmother. What if her grandmother was suddenly gone and she could not say goodbye? "I still do not think Grandma is old and that's why she can do it," interrupts Emma. "Grandma always manages everything. I'm going to tell her now that she's going to do a chemotherapy so she can recover!" Emma's mother sighs. She knows full well that when her daughter has something in her head, she tries everything to reach her goal. "In this case, unfortunately, it will not be possible!" she thinks. Emma is determined to drive the cancer away from her grandmother. "Besides, what does 'bad cancer' mean here? If someone is angry, he gets scolded and then he has to apologize. If you do not do that, I'll scold the cancer and then apologize and leave."

Outside the door she turns to her mother again, "Well, and so that's clear, if Grandma's cancer has apologized and gone, I'll scold Alois wife's cancer!" Without waiting for an answer, she knocks on the door and opens it. Determined, Emma enters the room.

In the hospital room

After the first three steps, she hesitates for a moment. She takes a deep breath. "Stay calm, Emma. This is just the Grandma with the bad cancer," she tries to encourage herself. "Grandma!" says Emma bravely. "Emma, my little angel! Let you look, my child." Emma's Grandma pushes her hand against the edge of the bed. Carefully, Emma approaches her grandma. Arriving at the bed, she thinks about giving her grandma a kiss on the cheek, as she always does. Grandma sees Emma's hesitation and so she just touches her hand. "It's good, my little one! I know that I do not look pretty anymore." Emma shakes her head, "No, that's not it." Emma thinks about what to say. Her usually so strong Grandma lies in front of her, pale and thin, in the nose a hose, on the body, a lot of tubes. Emma looks at the bubbling bottle over Grandma's head. Then to the monitors to the left of the bed. "I brought you a present," Emma says, handing Grandma a red scarf, adding, "Mama always says that you are so cold. You're not so cold anymore." Grandma smiles, "That's very nice of you, little one."

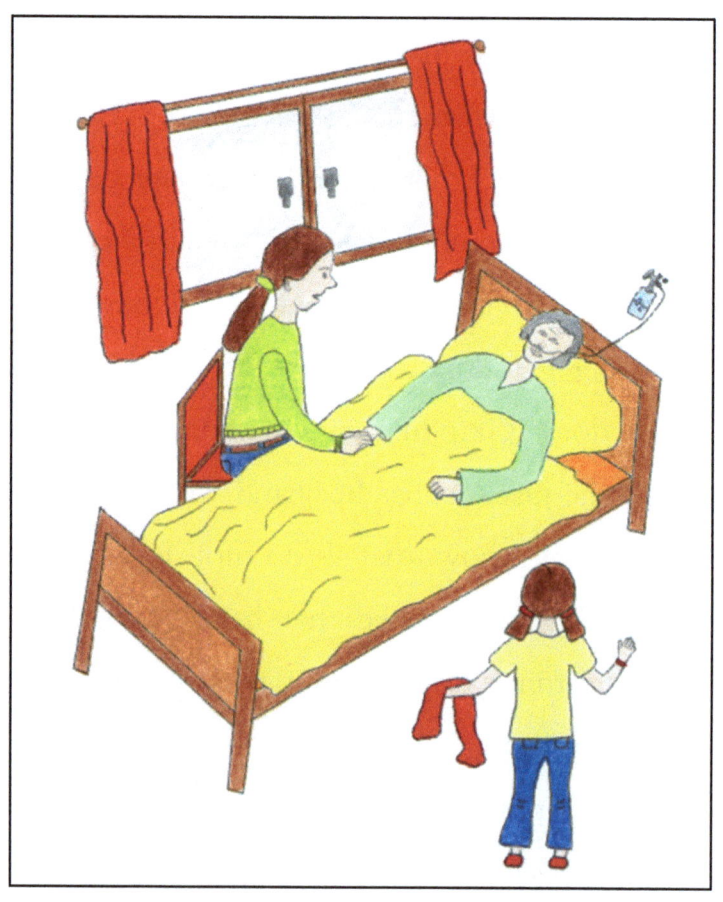

Emma looks again at the bubbling bottle. "Why do you have a hose in your nose, Grandma?" she dares to ask. "That's oxygen, Emma. You know, I cannot breathe so well." Emma raises her left eyebrow. "But Grandma, the tube is way too thin. No wonder you do not get enough air. You have to pull the hose out of your nose and then breathe like that. Look!" Emma breathes in and out deeply three times, pulling her shoulders up. "That's the way it works. And then you get a lot of air." Grandma smiles, "Oh Emma, you know, I have no more strength to breathe myself." Emma thinks, why do you need strength to breathe? "I do not understand that. I'm a lot smaller than you, and I do not have as much strength as Mom and Dad and you, but I can still breathe," says Emma irritated. "You know, Emma," her mother tries to explain, "you can imagine it as if you had a very bad cold. Then you also get air hardly and everything is too exhausting." Emma ponders, "So that means that

15

the evil cancer makes cold and therefore the nose is closed. And so that Grandma can breathe better, she has a tube in her nose, which passes through the cold. And that's why. It's because nasal drops are disgusting, right?" Mother desperately looks at Emma, "No, Emma, that's not the way it is." Emma puts her hands on her hips, "Yes, but then how is it?" she wants to know. "Oh, Emma, I cannot really explain it to you." Emma looks back and forth between her mother, her grandma and the hose. "Why can't you explain that? You are already big. Big people always know everything, and they can do everything," says Emma defiantly. Her mother shakes her head, "No, Emma, big people do not know everything, and they cannot do everything."

"But big people can cure the bad cancer, right?" Emma wants to know. "Sometimes they can, but sometimes they cannot," replies her mother. "When I grow up, I can cure the cancer," Emma

16

says with conviction. At that moment, the monitor next to the bed starts to beep loudly. Emma is startled. "Grandma, why is that beeping so loud?"

"That happens, little one, when the heart rate or the blood pressure goes too far," replies Grandma. "Heart rate … what is that?" Emma wonders. "You know that all people have a heart, Emma...," her mother begins. "And animals too," interrupts Emma. "Yes, animals, too. Anyway, the heart beats differently, depending on what you do. If you just sit still, it beats slower than if you run, for example. And when you sleep, it also beats differently," the mother tries to explain. "And Grandma's heart sleeps now?" Emma questions. "No, Emma, Grandma's heart did not sleep. A heart cannot sleep." Emma opens her eyes, "Oh…is a heart never tired?" she asks in astonishment. Her mother smiles, "No, Emma, a heart is never tired. When a heart cannot do it its work, it just stops, so it does not

17

sleep," she tries to explain. "Why is a heart never tired, and why does a heart never sleep? Does a heart need to eat and drink? How does it do it if it never stops? I should always sit down while eating and drinking. Does the heart not have a mom or dad who tells him to sit down...?"

"Oh, Emma," interrupts her mother. "I cannot really explain that to you," she says again. Emma puts her little hands on her hips again, "Well, then I'm looking for someone who can explain it to me correctly." Determined she goes to the door and is already in the hall, even before the mother can say something. "Emma, stay there!" she calls after her, but Emma is already gone.

In the doctor's room

In the hall, Emma looks left and right, with her right hand scratching her head, "When Mom and I went to Grandma's room, there were doctors in a room on the right side. We came from there," Emma points with her right index finger towards the exit, "so the doctors must be in that direction on the left side now," she says quietly to herself. Determined Emma walks down the hallway and looks through the open doors on the left side. Suddenly a doctor is standing in front of her and speaks to her, "Are you looking for something, young lady?" Frightened, Emma stops. "Yes, I'm looking for the doctor from my grandmother. Are you Grandma's doctor?" Emma wants to know. The doctor laughs, "This is possible if your grandma is here on the ward. What's your grandma's name?" she asks Emma. "My grandmother's name is Charlotte Katharina Neuberger, and I'm Emma Katharina Neuberger, and my grandmother has the bad cancer and does not have the strength to breathe. Now I want the bad cancer to go away," replies Emma. "And while you're at it, you can get rid of Alois' wife's cancer too, ok?" she adds. The doctor looks at Emma, "Who is Alois?"

"Alois is the man from the waiting room with the funny name. You see, I told him he has a weird name. But he is still nice. Anyway, his wife also has cancer. And he is certainly very angry because Alois looked pretty sad."

"Emma, there you are. You cannot just keep running like that. Excuse me, Doctor, my daughter just walked out of the room because she wanted to find someone who could answer all her questions," Emma's mother tries to explain. The doctor smiles, "So, you have questions." she turns to Emma. "Yes, quite a lot, but Mama cannot explain them to me," Emma pouts. "Well, if you want, I can maybe answer your questions," the doctor tries to comfort her. "Oh! That's great," Emma says happily. "But Doctor..."

"Wegemann is my name."

"My name is Misses Neuberger. It is nice to meet you," Emma's mother pleasantly holds out her hand to the doctor. "Please excuse the interruption. We do not want to stop you now," says her mother. "It's alright, you don't bother me." The doctor turns back to Emma, "If you want and your mom allows it, you can ask me anything you want to know." Emma looks at her mother. "Do you really think so?" her mother asks the doctor. "Of course!" the doctor smiles. "And my daughter will not bother you?"

"Certainly not," replies the doctor. "Alright, but you already know that little five-year-old girls can talk your ear off?" The doctor laughs, "That's no problem. We have great general and trauma surgeons in the clinic, so they can put it back." Now the mother has to laugh, too. Emma does not quite understand what the adults are talking about, but that does not matter, because she is very happy to have finally found someone who can answer all her questions. "If you want, Emma can come to the doctor's room and when we're done, I'll bring her back to you."

"And that's really alright?" her mother asks again. "Yes, that's really alright," confirms the doctor. The mother looks at Emma, "All right, you can stay with Doctor Wegemann, but only as long as she has time. And be nice to her, ok?"

"Ok!" Emma fidgets impatiently from excitement. "See you later," says her mother. "See you later," Emma and the doctor answer at the same time. They look back at Emma's mother, and they then go to the doctor's room.

"Would you like to sit down?" the doctor asks Emma. "Yes gladly. So, you are my Grandma's doctor?" Emma hesitates until she sits down properly. "Can you make Grandma healthy again?" she continues. The doctor briefly considers how to tell Emma that she can do nothing more for her grandma, except to make

22

her comfortable. "You cannot make her well, right?" interrupts Emma. "How did you know? I haven't responded," Doctor Wegemann replies. "If you could make Grandma healthy again, you should have said yes. But you did not say anything and that's why you cannot help Grandma anymore," Emma replies disappointed. "You are a very smart girl," notes the doctor. "My mom always says that, and Alois said that, too."

"Alois…that is the man from the waiting room, right?" the doctor asks. "Yes, that's right," confirms Emma. "Emma, do you know what your grandma has exactly?" the doctor asks. Emma looks quite surprised, "Yes, I know that, don't you?" Dr- Wegemann laughs, "Emma, I know it, I just wanted to know if you know that, too, so I can explain why we cannot help your grandma with more treatment."

"Oh, my Grandma has a stomach cancer, and he is very angry," says Emma. "Yes, that's right, the cancer started in the stomach, more specifically in the colon," the doctor tries to explain. Emma listens intently. "How did he get in there?" she wants to know. "You know, polyps sometimes grow in the gut..."

"Where is the intestine, and what are poly...polydings?" Emma interrupts the doctor. "Polyps are a kind of protuberance in the gut. Sometimes they look like little octopus or squid." Doctor Wegemann takes a sheet from the table and draws several polyps. "Look, that's what they look like," she says, handing the paper to Emma. "Actually, they look very funny," says Emma. "Yes, that's right, they look funny," confirms the doctor, "but if you do not remove them, they can get pretty angry," she adds. "Hmmm, and where is the intestine now?" asks Emma again. "The intestine is in your stomach," replies Doctor Wegemann. "And what does it look like?" Emma wants to know. "Come look at the wall. There is a chart hanging over there showing the

24

abdominal organs." Emma looks at the picture the doctor shows her. "That looks weird," she says confused. "That's the gut?" she asks. The doctor points to the middle of the picture. "Also, look, that's the small intestine and around the small intestine is the colon. And here in the large intestine, polyps grow," the doctor explains. "Hmmm, do all humans have these polydings?" Emma wants to know. "No, Emma, not all, but the older people get, the more often it happens. The polyps are in most cases quite harmless in the beginning. They just grow there. If you recognize them early through examinations, you can remove them and then everything is usually well again."

"And are the polydings already cancer?" Emma interrupts Doctor Wegemann. "No, not in the beginning, but they are growing. How long that takes can be very different. Some of them are very fast; others take a little longer," Doctor Wegemann continues. "Then Grandma had such polydings that then turned into a bad stomach cancer?" Emma tries to understand. "That's exactly how it was," confirms the doctor. "Where do the polydings come from, and why does it turn into a bad stomach cancer? Can't you do something to prevent them from coming?" Emma asks. "Well, actually our bodies are made up of lots of cells that are rebuilt on a regular basis. Depending on where the cells are and which cells they are, this happens at different rates. For example, the skin, the mucous membrane in the stomach, and the platelets need only a few days to weeks to regenerate, where the liver takes about two years to regenerate. The skeleton, or bone, takes about ten years and the muscles of the ribs can take even 15 years until it is newly formed." Emma thinks, "Does that mean then that I am sometimes completely remade?" The doctor laughs, "Hmmm, you could say that."

"Will I look different someday?" Emma wants to know. "No, it's not like that." The doctor thinks about how she can explain the process in the child's body to Emma. "Well, look, you've probably hurt yourself before, have not you?" "Yes, a few times already," confirms Emma. "The last time I stumbled over a branch at the stream, I really hurt myself a lot. My knee even bled, and the blood went through my pants," says Emma. "Yes, that certainly hurt a lot. Do you remember what happened after that, when it stopped bleeding?" Emma nods, "Yes, a scab formed where it bled. Mom said I should not take it off, but I wanted it gone, so I did not listen and scratched it off. It bled again."

"Well, you really should not do that." Doctor Wegemann winks, "But you know, adults do that, too." Emma looks surprised, *"Really?"* she would like to know. "Yes, really," confirms Doctor Wegemann. "But why not do that?" Emma wants to know. "On the one hand, evil germs can come in, and on the other, scars can happen. But depending on how you hurt yourself, scars are created anyway," admits the doctor with another wink. "Anyway, so a scab is formed. And if it fell off, or you scratched it off, what happens after that," the doctor asks from Emma. "Everything will be fine after that," explains Emma. "Exactly, the cells have split, and you have beautiful, healthy skin on your knee again." Emma asks in astonishment, "So that's how it works?" "That's exactly how it works," confirms the doctor. "Can you tell me if your knee looks different now than it did before?" the doctor asks. Emma shakes her head, "No, my knee looks as usual."

"That's a good thing. That's the way it should be." The doctor continues, "Do you know what I mean by that?" Emma thinks hard, "The cells keep growing over and over again, even if you hurt yourself. They'll just come back…" Emma thinks even harder, "If the new comes and my knee looks like always…," Emma begins to radiate, "then I do not look any different, when all the cells are new."

"Great, that's what I was after! You are really smart for being such a little girl," says the doctor impressed. Emma laughs with joy at her performance, but then she gets serious again. "Does that mean that the polydings and the bad cancer are also cells?" she wants to know. "Yes, Emma, it is like that. New cells are constantly growing in the body. Normally this happens very peacefully. But sometimes there are cells that grow too fast, or that change so that they are evil," the doctor tries to explain to Emma. "And that's the bad cancer then?" Emma asks sadly. "Yes, that's the bad cancer," confirms the doctor sympathetically. After a moment of silence, Emma asks, "How do the cells get angry?" The doctor sighs, "It happens in very different ways. Ultimately, however, something breaks in the cells when they are re-formed."

"Can I also get cancer?" Emma is curious. The doctor swallows. How can she now explain to Emma that theoretically anyone can get cancer without frightening her? Emma notes that the doctor does not know what to say. "So, I can get cancer, too?" Emma says softly. "You know, Emma, everyone can theoretically get cancer," Doctor Wegemann admits honestly. "The likelihood, however, is much lower than that of stumbling over a branch quite often. And honestly … you are still too young to get cancer. Look how old your grandma is and look how old you are."

"Yes, my Grandma is older than me. That's right," confirms Emma. "And Alois' wife, too," she adds. "Well, you see," the doctor tries to cheer up Emma. Emma thinks, "May I ask you another question?" "Of course, you can! What else do you want to know?" the doctor encourages Emma to ask. "My Grandma doesn't want to do chemotherapy, and they don't tell me

30

why." The doctor smiles, "Chemotherapy, you know, this is a very powerful drug that runs through the body. The patients who get this become very weak..."

"And they lose their hair," Emma interrupts the doctor. "Yes, exactly, you lose your hair as a result," she confirms. In any case, there are patients who are already so weak that they no longer want treatment. Most of the time, it is patients for whom the cancer is very advanced and treatment would have little chance of success," the doctor tries to explain. "What does 'advanced' mean?" Emma questions. "This means that the cancer is already very large and has usually gone elsewhere."

"Has Grandma's cancer already gone elsewhere?" The doctor nods, "Yes, Emma, it has."

"And where did he go?" Emma wonders. The doctor briefly considers whether she can tell Emma the truth.

At that moment there is a knock on the door. "Yes, please?" says Doctor Wegemann towards the door. Emma's mother looks inside and says, "Excuse me, Doctor. I just wanted to check on Emma."

"Hello, Mum! I'm fine, and it's a lot of fun with the doctor," Emma laughs. "Well, you also found someone who listens to you for a long time, you little chatterbox." Emma's mother also laughs. "I'm not a chatterbox," says Emma stubbornly, crossing her arms in front of her chest. "Emma just asked me where the cancer has already spread, but I wasn't sure how to answer the question because of the confidentiality," the doctor turns to Emma's mother. "I understand," Emma's mother says as she turns to Emma. "Emma, Grandma's cancer is already in the liver and lungs. They…"

"No, you shouldn't tell me that," Emma exclaims. "The doctor should explain that to me," Emma says, covering her ears. "Emma,

Doctor Wegemann has to keep working now. You can't stop her all the time, you know?" Emma's mother says. Emma starts to cry, "But we are not done yet. You should go back to Grandma." The doctor looks at Emma with pity and then turns to the mother, "It's just a family consultation. Emma is a relative," she smiles. "Yes, but don't you have to talk to other relatives?" Emma's mother asks. The doctor shakes her head, "No, no one has contacted me yet," she replies. "Very well, Emma, you can still stay." Still sad and somewhat angry, Emma just pouts without answering her mother. "I'll take her to the room afterwards when we're done," the doctor says trying to ease the situation. "Thank you!" Emma's mother replies and turns to the door to go out. As soon as the mother has closed the door behind her, Emma continues, "Are the lungs there for breathing?" she wants to know. "Yes, something like that," confirms the doctor. "We breathe in the air. It goes into the lungs. Then the lungs absorb the oxygen and release it into the blood. At the same time, they give off what we consume when we exhale, that is, carbon dioxide." Emma thinks, "There is oxygen in Grandma's bubble bottle?"

"Yes, that's true. Your grandma needs oxygen because the cancer means she can't breathe enough," Doctor Wegemann affirms. "Can you hear breathing in the lungs?" Emma asks. The doctor nods, "Yes, you can hear the breathing." She thinks, "You have been to the pediatrician, haven't you?" Emma nods, "Yes, but he is very angry!" The doctor looks startled. "Why is he so bad?" she asks. "Well, because he always pricks me off." The doctor laughs, "Yes, unfortunately, that is sometimes a part of it," she says. She takes the stethoscope out of her coat pocket and sits back on the chair. "Have you been bugged before?" Emma laughs. "Yes, I know that. You can hear the heart with it," she says. "Right. Have you ever heard your heart before?" the doctor
34

questions Emma. Emma shakes her head, "No, I have not yet," she replies. "If you want, you can do it now," Doctor Wegemann offers. "Oh yes, please," Emma says. Doctor Wegemann puts the earplugs in her ears and puts the chest piece on Emma's chest.

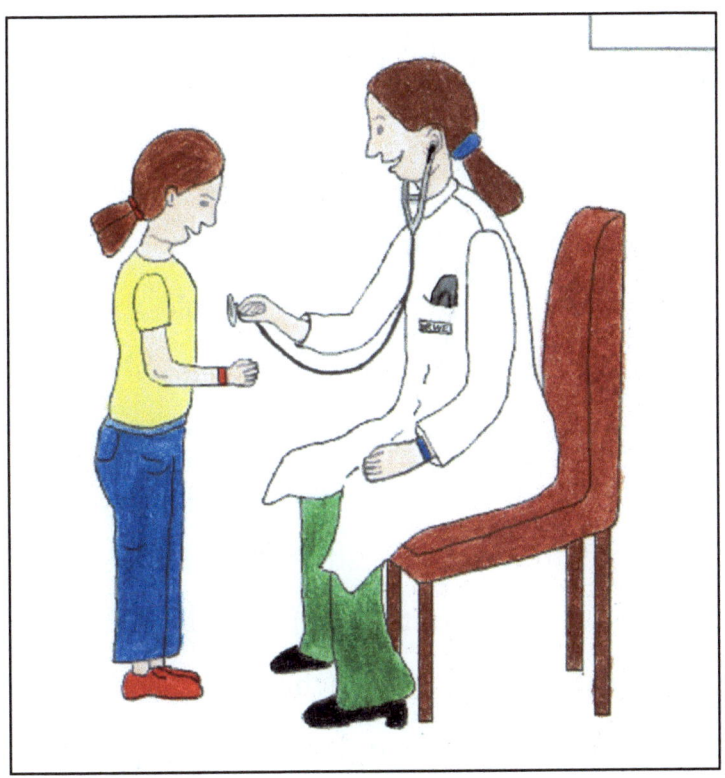

"A healthy, strong heart, as it should be," she says, handing Emma the earplugs. Carefully, Emma pokes the earplugs in her ears. Astonished, she looks at the doctor. "Oh … that sounds like *that*?" Doctor Wegemann laughs, "Yes, the heart sounds like that," she confirms. At the same time, she is a bit touched by Emma's reaction. For her the beating of the heart is a natural sound, but for Emma it is something completely new. "And where can I hear my breath now?" Emma interrupts Doctor Wegemann's mind. "We have to hold the chest piece on your back," she says, placing the chest piece between Emma's left shoulder blade and spine. "Now you have to take a deep breath in and out of the mouth", she tells Emma. Emma breathes in and out so powerfully that her shoulders go up a few inches and then lower again. "Do you hear something?" Doctor Wegemann wants to know. "That sounds like the wind that is sometimes at my window in the

36

evening," Emma answers. Doctor Wegemann laughs again, "That's a nice description. That's the sound of lungs that are healthy."

"Can you listen to me, please?" asks Emma and gives the doctor the earplugs. "Naturally! Take another deep breath in and out!" the doctor invites Emma. After six breaths, she looks at Emma and says, "Everything's all right, young lady." Emma smiles, "I'm glad." After a moment's hesitation, Emma asks, "May I hear your heart, too?"

"But of course," the doctor gives Emma the earplugs again and places the chest piece inside over her left breast. "Oh...that's a lot slower than mine," says Emma. "That's right. Your heart beats about 95 to 100 times a minute. For me, it is between 60 and 80 beats per minute."

"Is that bad that your heart is slower than mine?" Emma wants to know. The doctor smiles, "No, Emma, that's completely normal. This has to do with the body surface. Each smaller the body, the more the heart has to work, so that the body is supplied with enough blood and oxygen," she tries to explain. "That's quite complicated, I think." The doctor nods affirmatively. "I think I have to go back to my mom, otherwise she'll come back to find me," says Emma. "Alright, I'll take you to her. It was fun with you, Emma," the doctor tells her. "I thought it was very nice, and thank you for explaining and showing me so much," Emma says. "I liked doing that," Doctor Wegemann says.

Together, they leave the doctor's room and walk down the hall towards the patient room. Emma's footsteps slow down. The doctor notices Emma's hesitation and looks at her, "Are you alright?" she asks worriedly. Emma nods, "I am, but Grandma is not." Emma ponders, "Does Grandma really have to die?" she asks. The doctor sighs softly and squats to look Emma in the eyes. "Unfortunately, yes, little one," she says helplessly. Emma closes her eyes. A tear runs down her right cheek. "May I hug you?" the doctor asks carefully. Without answering, Emma throws herself into the doctor's arms and begins to cry. After some time, Emma wipes her cheeks, looks at the doctor and says. "I am better now. Thank you. We can go now." Touched by Emma's reaction, the doctor strokes her gently on the head. Together, they continue along the corridor. At the door, Emma stops and looks at the doctor again, "And you are sure that you cannot help my Grandma anymore?" she asks softly. The doctor nods, "Yes, Emma, I'm quite sure," she answers just as softly. Emma thinks, "I'm thinking hard. Maybe I can remember some good medicine for my Grandma," she says with conviction. "If I found something, may I call you then?" The doctor nods, "You can, brave little girl." Emma thanks her and knocks on the door. As she walks in, she turns around again, "Thank you, nice doctor." The doctor smiles, "Thank you, little girl." With these words, Emma disappears into the room and closes the door behind her. The doctor sighs again, turns around and goes back to the doctor's room. On the way, she thinks all the time of the little girl, who is convinced she can help her grandmother.

The herb garden

In the evening Emma searches her entire closet and the shelf. "I got an herbal book from Grandma," she says quietly to herself. "There's got to be a plant in there that I can use to help Grandma with medicine." Emma is so engrossed, she did not notice her mother coming into the room. "Emma, what are you doing?" she asks confused. Emma startled, "I'm looking for the herbal book, Grandma gave me for a birthday," she replies. "What do you need that for?" her mother wants to know. "I need this because I want to make Grandma medicine against the bad stomach cancer," says Emma with conviction. "Oh, Emma, come here!" The mother sits down on the bed and asks Emma to sit next to her. "Emma, you cannot help Grandma anymore. Chemotherapy is the strongest remedy for cancer, but even that would not help anymore," the mother tries to explain to Emma. Emma gets angry, "Maybe you and the dear doctor cannot help Grandma anymore, but I will be able to help Grandma because I really want that. And if you do not want to help Grandma anymore, then that's really mean. If you had bad stomach cancer, then I would help you and not just let you die!" Frightened by Emma's reaction, the mother tries to explain," Emma, I do not want to let Grandma die, and I would help her if I somehow could, but I cannot do anything." "But you can at least try it!" With these words, Emma turns back to the shelf and throws book after book on the floor. The mother just sits in silence and looks at the ever-growing pile of books. Finally, Emma finds the herbal book. Satisfied, she goes to bed with it. "May I please lie down and read in my book now?" she asks angrily. "But, Emma, you cannot read yet," the mother replies in surprise. "I can do that. Can you please leave my room now?" Sadly, the mother gets up from the bed. "Can I at least give

42

you a good night kiss?" she asks Emma exhausted. Emma hesitates, "Okay, but I'm still mad at you." The mother leans over to Emma and gives her a good night kiss on the cheek. "Sleep well, my little one," she says softly. "Good night!" replies Emma and sits down on her bed, even before the mother has left the room, and begins to leaf through her book. Two hours later, Emma falls asleep. At night, however, she sleeps very restlessly. Again, and again she wakes up because she dreams that her Grandma is already dead. Only toward morning does she falls exhaustedly into a deep sleep.

After Emma got up, washed, dressed and had breakfast, she went out into the garden with her herbal book. Her Grandma had lovingly designed the garden and created and planted the most varied flowers, plants and herb beds. Emma has always helped her and so she already has learned a lot about the flowers, plants and herbs. Emma remembers that her Grandma said that the Native Americans have many medicinal plants and make medicine out of them. Unfortunately, they have never talked about what makes the Native Americans' medicine against cancer. Emma kneels in front of one of the herb beds and opens her book. She tries to compare the herbs from the bed with the illustrations in the book. After some time, she found most of the herbs, but since she cannot read, she does not know which herbs they are and what they can be used for or how. So, she just decides to pick some herbs and plants and put them next to the book. She walks into the house to pick up the phone. Back in the garden, she wants to call the doctor from the hospital, but she remembers that she does not know what the name of the hospital is or the number. Emma does not want to ask her mother because she would definitely ban it. Emma thinks for a moment and then decides to call 911. "Mum and dad always say I should ring

911 in an emergency, and this is an emergency," she says as she dials the number.

"Emergency Fire and Rescue Service. Where is the emergency site?"

"Hello, this is Emma Katharina Neuberger, and I urgently need to talk to the lovely doctor from the hospital."

"Emma, where are you?" asks the gentleman from the rescue center. "I'm at home," replies Emma. "And is there an emergency at your home?" the emergency dispatcher wants to know. "Yes, because my grandma has cancer, and I have to help her now," says Emma desperately. "Where is your grandma? Can she answer the phone?" Emma shakes her head, "No, my grandma is in the hospital."

"I see. Your grandma is in the hospital because she has cancer, and you are at home and want to help her now. Is that correct?"

"Yes exactly. Can you please help me now?" Emma pleads. "I can try, but I have to change the line for a while. Could you please stay tuned? I'll answer the phone right away," the emergency dispatcher says.

"It's good, I'm waiting."

"You will hear a melody for a moment, ok?"

"Yes, that's good."

After a few seconds the emergency dispatcher is on the phone again.

"Emma, are you still there?" he asks.

"Yes, I'm here," replies Emma. "It's good. Now tell me the story again in peace," the emergency dispatcher instructs. "Well, my grandma has a bad stomach cancer, and the doctors cannot help her anymore, and my mom does not want to help her, so I have to do that now. You know, my grandma is not supposed to die," explains Emma. "Understood, and how do you want to help your grandma now?" he asks. "I got a birthday herb from my grandma, and now I've

46

searched for the herbs and plants in the book we have in the garden. I want to make medicine out of it for Grandma...," Emma hesitates, "but ... but I cannot read. I'm only five," she says sadly. "There you have something very serious," says the emergency dispatcher on the phone. "Are you sure that can work?" he wants to know. "Yes, that will work because my Grandmother tells me the Native Americans always make medicine. All I have to do now is know which herbs and plants to use to make the medicine for the cancer," explains Emma. "What does your mom say that you want to make medicine?" the emergency dispatcher asks. "I do not want to talk to my mom. I'm mad at her because she says Grandma is dying, and she just does not care." "Understood. Is your mom home now?" "Yes, but she does not know that I got on the phone to call you. And I have to talk to the lovely doctor from the hospital right now. She said that if I came up with a medicine, I could call her."

"And now you want to ask her about the herbs and plants, right?"

"Yes exactly. But I do not know the phone number, so I cannot call there."

"And because you know 911, you've called us now so we can help you out, right?" Emma nods, "Exactly because it's an emergency, and Mom and Dad always say I should call 911 in an emergency," replies Emma. The emergency dispatcher laughs, "You did very well, little girl," he encourages Emma. "So, let's see what I can do for you. Do you know which hospital your grandma is in?" asks the emergency dispatcher. Emma shakes her head, "No, all I know is that it's a big hospital," she replies. "Okay, you know where you live," the emergency dispatcher continues. "Yes, I live in Nideggen." "Good, then Düren is probably the answer. Have you heard of this place before?"

"Yeah, Mama has said that a few times," says Emma. "Ok, now there are three hospitals in Düren two of them with the Department of Oncology. Since one is a medical office, I think I know which is the hospital. Hmmm...look, what's your grandmother's name?" the emergency dispatcher asks. "My grandma is Charlotte Katharina Neuberger," replies Emma. "Well, I'll try something out for you now, and you'll just stay on the line again and listen to the melody, ok?" Emma nods, "Yeah, that's good. I'll do that," she replies.

After a minute, the emergency dispatcher is back on the line.

"Emma, I have good news for you. I know where your grandma is."
"Oh, that's great," Emma says happily. "I'll connect you to the clinic now. You just stay tuned until someone's on the line, ok?"

"Yes, I'll do it. But…what if the call goes away? Sometimes that just happens," Emma asks. "I will stay on the line until you're connected, and if anything goes wrong, I'll call you back, agreed?" replies the emergency dispatcher. "Yeah, but you do not have my number," says Emma, surprised. The emergency dispatcher laughs, "Yes, I can see it in the display. The emergency center and the police can always see who is still on the phone," he explains to Emma. "Oh, I did not know that," she replies.

"See you then, Emma."

"See you, and thanks for your help!"

"I liked being able to do that," replies the emergency dispatcher.

"Central, Hospital Düren, Weniger on the phone, good day," answers Mister Weniger, the hospital telephone operator. "Hello. This is Emma Katharina Neuberger. I would like to speak with my grandma's doctor, please," says Emma.

"Emma, I've heard of you," replies a friendly voice on the phone. "Your grandmother is here with us on the oncology floor, and you would like to speak Doctor Wegemann. Is that correct?" Mister Weniger would like to know.

"Unfortunately, I do not know what the doctor's name is," replies Emma, "but she is very nice, and she has explained a lot to me."

"Hmmm, I'll try to ring her. Please wait."

"Alright, I'm waiting. I already know that from the man at the fire department," says Emma.

Mister Weniger laughs, "Ok, see you soon."

After a few seconds, he is back on the line again. "Emma, Doctor Wegemann is now on the line, and I will hang up, ok?"

"Yes, it's fine. Thanks!" Emma responds.

"Wegemann. Hello, Emma," the doctor begins. "Hello, dear doctor, I have found something to help Grandma, but I cannot read. Can you please help me?" Emma wants to know. "So, tell me, what did you find?" the doctor asks affectionately. "I got an herb book from Grandma for my birthday, and now I'm looking at our herbs and plants from the garden. I found all of them, and now all I have to do is get the medicine to help Grandma recover, "explains Emma excitedly. "Oh, Emma, that's very nice of you, that you're trying…," the doctor does not know how to tell the truth to Emma when she has so much hope. "Now, if I tell you what the herbs and plants look like, can you please tell me which one to make the medicine for the cancer?" Emma asks. The doctor wipes a few tears from her cheeks, so touched by the brave little girl. "Emma, I really would love to help you, but I do not know how. I do not know any plant that can cure the cancer. You know, chemotherapy is the strongest thing that is currently available for cancer and if it does not help…" the doctor hesitates for a moment, "then it cannot be done

52

with a plant," she continues. Emma starts to cry, "Are you sure about that?"

"Yes, unfortunately," the doctor confirms. Both are silent for a moment. "Do you not think that maybe I can invent a medicine? Maybe you do not even know that a certain plant can help against the cancer or a few together?" Emma asks as a last hope. "Yes, maybe plants one day can help, but right now it's hopeless, little one," the doctor says softly. Emma hesitates, then she says, "Alright... then I'll think of something else. See you soon, dear doctor."

"See you soon, little Emma", the doctor answers sadly.

The letter

In the evening, Emma sits at dinner and still thinks about how she can help her grandmother. She realizes there is no point in being angry with the cancer. "So, I have to come up with something new," she thinks. "You're still angry, aren't you?" her mother asks carefully. Emma mulls over what she's been thinking about, "Could be," she replies quietly, biting into her tomato bread.

Later in bed, Emma thinks for a long time. Suddenly she has an idea. She jumps up, tears open the drawers from her desk, and takes out her paper and her pencil case. She goes to the door and looks through the crack in the door, but she cannot see or hear anything. Carefully she opens her door and walks slowly down the hall. She sneaks toward her parents' bedroom. Once there, she hears a quiet, steady and calm breathing. "Dumb, mom and dad seem to be sleeping," she says, trotting back to her room. She looks out the window. The moon is high in the sky. Slowly she walks back to her bed and lies down again. "Then I'll have to wait until tomorrow," she says and snuggles deep into her blanket. After a few minutes, Emma falls asleep, too.

After breakfast, Emma gets a note and a pen from her room and hands it over to her mother. "Mom, can you please write me a letter?" she asks her mother. "A letter? Who do you want to write?" her mother asks surprised. "To the bad cancer. I want to write that he should go away and leave my grandma alone," replies Emma. The mother sighs. Actually, she would like to tell Emma that it does not work, but she does not want her to get angry again. Instead, she takes the sheet and pen and sits down at the kitchen table. "All right, what do you want to write?" she asks.

56

Satisfied, Emma sits next to her mother. "Obviously, Mama has changed her mind and now wants to help, too," she thinks and is happy about it. "Please write: Bad belly cancer…," Emma ponders, "No, better not write 'bad belly cancer', otherwise he is still angry and does not listen to me," she says determined. "That could be," replies her mother. "Good, then please write: Dear belly cancer, I'm Emma Katharina Neuberger, and my grandmother is Charlotte Katharina Neuberger. I am five years old and love my grandma very much. Unfortunately, you have now grown up in my grandma and then got angry. I do not know why you did that because my grandma is very nice. It would be very nice of you if you would go again because my grandmother has to die otherwise. I would be very sad about it, and my grandma also is determined. So, can you please go away? Sincerely," Emma. During the dictation, Emma made small breaks again and again, so that her mother could write down everything. After her mother is finished, Emma beams at her, takes the sheet, and thanks her. "Thank you, Mama! I'll go to my room and copy the letter." Emma's just out the door when her mother calls her back, "Emma?"

"Yes, mom?" replies Emma and looks into the kitchen. "You know that you have to send a letter. Where do you want to send your letter?" asks her mother with interest. Emma thinks, "That's easy," she says resolutely, "if the cancer lives in Grandma's stomach, then the letter must also in Grandma's stomach!"

"*What?* How is the letter supposed to get in there?" the mother asks her confusedly. "Well, very simple, Mom, Grandma just has to eat the letter," Emma replies, turning around and going to her room.

Once there, Emma sits at the desk and begins to copy the letter neatly. After 40 minutes, she is ready. She thinks about whether she should decorate the letter nicely, so that the cancer is pleased with her letter. She looks at her crayons and decides to color a beautiful flower meadow on the letter. "The cancer will be happy about it," she says quietly and is happy about her great idea.

After Emma finishes, she goes to the kitchen and shows her mother the letter. "Look, Mom, I'm done. Do you like it?" she asks eagerly. Her mother takes the letter from her and looks at it for a long time. "You really have made it very nice, little one," she praises Emma. "Thank you, Mama! Now all I need is an envelope and a stamp. Can you please give that to me?" Emma asks her mother. Her mother turns to the kitchen table, "I have already laid out everything for you," she says and hands the things to Emma. After Emma has finished everything, she looks at her mother happily, "Now Grandma only has to eat the letter and then everything is fine again," she rejoices. "That's how we will do it, Emma," the mother replies, wondering secretly how that is going to end.

Alois

In the afternoon Emma returns to the hospital with her mother. Emma is very excited because she wants to give the letter to the cancer. She has held the letter in her hands the entire drive so that it will not get lost. In the hall in front of the ward, they meet a friend of the mother. The two adults start a conversation. "May I go ahead, please?" Emma asks her mother excitedly. Her mother nods, "It's good, little one, you know which room is Grandma's."

"Thanks!" Emma replies and down the hall.

"Not so fast, Emma," the mother calls after her, but Emma is already gone. She walks so fast that she almost collides with Doctor Wegemann, who is just coming from her office. "Yikes, Emma, you're fast," she says. "Hello, dear doctor. I have to go to my grandma very quickly. I have to give her a letter for the bad stomach cancer," says Emma. "A letter?" the doctor asks in astonishment. "Yes, I wrote the bad stomach cancer and told him to go away please. And now I have to give Grandma the letter quickly so she can eat it," explains Emma. "Your grandma should what?" the doctor asks even more surprised. "Well, the cancer is still in Grandma's stomach, so for him to get the letter, Grandma has to eat it," says Emma very excited as she jumps up and down. The doctor scratches her head, "Emma, I'm not so sure if..." At that moment, Alois comes out of his wife's room. Emma sees that Alois is very sad. "Look, there's Alois... He looks very sad. Do you know what he has?" Emma asks the doctor. At that moment, Emma has a very bad feeling. She runs as fast as she can and she throws herself at him clasping his legs. "Alois, why are you so sad?" asks Emma carefully. "Do you feel pain?" Alois strokes Emma's hair, then he kneels down in front of her, "Oh, Emma..." he says softly and starts to cry. "Why are you crying, Alois?"

"My dear Erna... she is dead," Alois sobbed. Emma swallows, "But why? Did the evil cancer kill her?" Emma asks. "Yes, little one, the bad cancer has killed her," Alois confirms. Emma looks at the letter she has placed next to her. "Maybe I should have written a letter to Alois's wife's bad cancer, too," she thinks. Alois wipes his eyes. "Wait, Alois, I have a tissue for you," says Emma and pulls one out from her pants pocket. Carefully, she holds it out to him.

"Thanks, little one!" Alois takes the handkerchief and wipes his eyes. "Do you want one more?" asks Emma. "I have a lot of them," she adds, pointing to the package. "That's enough for me. Thank you, Emma."

Alois looks at the envelope. "Did you paint your grandma a picture?" he asks Emma. Emma shakes her head. She does not dare tell Alois what's in the envelope. Somehow it suddenly feels stupid to have written a letter to cancer. Alois sees Emma slowly pushing the letter under her knees. "Did I say something wrong?" Alois asks uncertainly. Emma shakes her head again, "No, that's not it," Emma hesitates for a moment, "I wrote a letter to the bad cancer in Grandma's stomach and told him to leave," she adds softly. Alois smiles, "That's nice, little one. You have come up with something good," he encourages Emma. Emma lowers her head, "But it will not help," she says sadly. Alois sighs. He would like to tell Emma that everything is going to be ok again and that her grandmother is recovering. He knows that's not true. As if reading his mind, Emma looks at Alois and asks, "Is Grandma going to die?" Alois begins to cry again. "The cancer is evil. I hate him!" Emma says angry and begins to cry too. Angry, she takes the letter and tears it into several small pieces. Alois sits silently beside her. Emma's mother, who has just come into the hall, sees her daughter and hurries to her. Halfway there, however, she is held back by Doctor Wegemann.

"Misses Neuberger, no." Emma's mother stops and looks questioningly at the doctor, "What do you think, Doctor?"

"I think Emma understands that there is no chance for her grandmother," replies the doctor. Her mother looks at Emma, "Do you really think so?" The doctor nods, "I think so," she replies. "I would suggest you leave them alone." Emma's mother nods uncertainly. "Well, if you think so," she agrees. "Yes. Come on, let's go over the other station. I think Emma will come when she's done," the doctor suggests. Emma's mother hesitates for a moment, then she says, "Alright, I trust you. She will not be lost in the hospital and maybe it's good for her. She's very angry lately and is trying hard to save her grandmother." The doctor nods, "Yes, I know."

Together they go to the other station.

After tearing up the letter, Emma looks at Alois and asks softly, "Alois, does it hurt to die?" Alois thinks, "Sometimes yes...sometimes not," he answers exhausted. "Does it Grandma hurts dying?" Emma wants to know. Alois shakes his head, "No, Emma, your grandma does not hurt. She's getting strong meds, you know?" Emma sobbing, "But it hurts me! It hurts me here!" says Emma, pointing to her heart. "I know Emma, it hurts me here, too, with Erna!" Alois also points to his heart. Both of them are crying. "If

Grandma is dead, then I can never talk to her again. I can never pick flowers with her again and never go back to the lake with her. Grandma likes the lake. Grandma just will be gone, and I'll forget everything because people forget things when they have not seen someone for a while," Emma sobs. Alois strokes Emma's hair, "You know, little one" he says, "as long as you think about all the nice things you've done with your grandmother and do not forget her, your grandma will not be gone. She will live in you, in your heart. Forgotten is only someone you no longer think about," Alois tries to comfort Emma. "But I can't see Grandma anymore, and I can't talk to her anymore. What if I forget what she looks like?" Emma asks. "It's normal for the memories to fade at some point, Emma, but they'll never go away completely. And you will have pictures of your grandmother. They will remind you how your grandma looked," Alois replies. "But I can't talk to her anymore," Emma says softly. "Yes, you can. And you know something, Emma? Your grandma will even talk to you," Alois tries to encourage Emma. Emma looks quite surprised, "How can Grandma talk to me?" she wants to know. "You'll feel it someday, little one. Maybe not in the near future. But eventually you feel it. And then you will know that your grandma is with you. Of course, she will not really be there talking to you, but you'll feel like your grandma is with you," explains Alois. "I'm afraid I'm still too young to understand that, Alois," Emma says quietly. "That does not matter, little one," answers Alois and gently strokes Emma's hair again. "Come on," he says, "I'll take you to your grandma. You should use the time to remember beautiful things with your grandmother. It will do you good and your grandma, too," says Alois smiling and holds out his hand to Emma. "Did you do that to your wife, too?" Emma wants to know. "Oh, yes. We talked a lot," says Alois. "What about?" asks

Emma. "We talked about how we got to know each other, how I proposed marriage to her in the hayloft, how we got married, and what our first shared apartment looked like." Emma listens intently. "We remembered our holidays at the lake and our first car. But we also talked about how sad we were back then because we could not have children. Yes, we talked about all these things," says Alois. "Did that make you sad?" Emma asks. "It is certainly very sad when you talk about things and know that you can never do that again." Alois nods, "Yes, it makes you very sad, but it also helps to deal with the pain, you know?" Emma nods. "Then I'll tell stories to Grandma, too," says Emma determined. "That's nice," answers Alois. Together they walk to her grandma's room.

Memories with Grandma

"Emma, my little angel," says Grandma in a weak voice. "I am very happy to see you again." Emma thinks she should tell her grandmother that they can see each other quite often. Emma decides not to say so. She thinks of Alois and what he told her. "Is something wrong, Emma?" the mother asks. Emma takes a deep breath, "But... I just thought of something," she replies. "What?" the mother wants to know. "Alois just told me that he and his wife liked to be at the lake. Do you remember, Grandma, how we always were at the lake?" Emma tries to start with her memories. "At lake? But of course, my child. I remember that very well," says Grandma. "You taught me to swim in the lake," says Emma. "Yes, that's true. In the beginning, you were very afraid to learn to swim and did not really want to. At some point we played in the lake with your ball and went further into the water."

"Yeah, and then I just stood on my toes, and you threw the ball a little further into the water."

"You were so scared to lose your beloved red ball that you voluntarily swam after it, without actually being able to do it," Grandma laughs. "Yes, I could do it all at once," confirms Emma. Suddenly Emma laughs loudly, "Do you remember how you fell into the lake with all your things because you looked back when we played catch?"

"How could I forget that? You laughed so hard while I sat like a drowned poodle in the water," said Grandma. "You looked really funny," chuckles Emma. "Oh, and then we ate the delicious marble cake we baked earlier, remember?" asks Emma. "Yes, I remember," confirms Grandma. "Grandpa pretended to be grumpy because he was not allowed to lick the raw dough off the spoons. But you know,

Grandpa tried again and again. But he did not once," says Grandma. Emma laughs, "Yes, that's just what you remember. Grandpa always licked something out of the bowl when you put the cake in the oven." "Grandpa got something?" Grandma says with pretend outrage. "Oh, Grandma, you surely know that. You've always seen, when I've got the chocolate from the candy jar when I was always very quiet." Now Grandma laughs, "Children and grandpas are never quiet when it comes to snacking." Emma pulls one pout, "But that's sooo delicious," she says. "Until you get a stomachache, out of sheer snacking, right?" asks Grandma. Emma looks down and paints a circle on the floor with her right foot. "Well, you'll remember the cookies we baked every Christmas. Two years ago, you ate so many cookies and sugar sprinkles that you got really sick afterwards." Emma shakes herself, "Oh, I remember that. That was pretty disgusting."

Grandma winks, "It will not have been that bad, but you just kept eating the next day," she laughs. Emma thinks, "This Christmas, I got a nice doll from you and Grandpa with a doll carriage." The grandmother nods, "Yes, you always drove around with your doll Lisa," she agrees. "Last year you got a bike. In the summer I wanted to teach you how to ride without training wheels," said Grandma wistfully. "But Grandma, you can always do that," Emma ponders, "Oh, actually I would like to wait a bit with it," Emma swindles. "Actually, one should not swindle, but grandma should not be sad," Emma thinks desperately. Grandma sees that Emma feels uncomfortable. "Alright, little one, I know what you're thinking right now," she says softly. Emma starts crying. "Grandma, I don't want you to die!" she says desperately. Grandma strokes Emma's hair gently, "But child, everyone must die one day. And I am already old and so sick. It's not nice to be sick and suffering. It's a salvation for me," she tries to comfort Emma. "Not for me," says Emma softly. "Are not you afraid to die, Grandma?" Emma wants to know. "No, my child, I'm not," Grandma answers with satisfaction. "What happens when you're dead?" she asks carefully. "You know, Emma, everyone thinks something different. Some believe that we will continue in some form thereafter. That you go to heaven or are born again. Others believe that nothing will come afterwards," she tries to explain. "And what do you think?" Emma asks. "I believe that afterwards I am completely free, have no more pain, and see all the people who have already died."

"Also Grandpa?" Emma asks. Grandma nods, "Yes, also grandpa," she says with a smile. But what if it's not true and nothing happens after that?"

"You know, Emma, that's okay, too. I will not know anymore then. It will be ok for me." Emma looks irritated, "I don't understand. How can things go well when you have to die?" Grandma nods understandingly, "I'll explain it to you. Now I'm sick I have a lot of pain without medication, and cannot do anything except lie in bed. When I die, I'm free. I imagine that when I'm dead, I will see all the people I love and have lost again. So, I'm looking forward to it."

"Yes, but if it's not so," interrupts Emma her grandma. "Then it's not bad because I then no longer know," Grandma tries to explain. "Now I understand," says Emma, "it's kind of a nice idea." Together, they remember many more stories they experienced. When evening came, Emma did not want to go. She has the feeling that if she leaves, she will not see her grandma again. Emma looks at the monitors that have been beeping the last few hours again and again. Somehow, they seem to confirm Emma's fears. Grandma sees Emma's hesitation. Carefully, she takes her hand. "It's all right, Emma. We'll meet again...someday," she says softly. "Promise?"

76

"Promise," Grandma replies. Slowly, Emma goes to the door. She turns around again and waves. Grandma raises her hand with her last strength and waves to Emma. "Take care, my little angel!" Emma sighs. She leaves the room with her mother. After a few steps, however, Emma turns around and runs back. She opens the door, throws herself into her grandmother's arms and begins to cry terribly. "Don't go, Grandma. Please don't go," she says in tears. "It's all right, little one, it's all right," Grandma tries to reassure Emma. "If I go now, I'll never see you again I feel it," Emma sobs. Grandma doesn't answer. Instead, she gently strokes Emma's hair. After some time, Emma looks at her grandmother, "Please do not forget me, Grandma," she whispers softly. Grandma shakes her head, "I could never forget such a sweet girl like you," she replies affectionately.

Two days later, Doctor Wegemann calls to tell them that Grandma has gone peacefully.

Funeral

"Emma, are you coming to eat, please?" her mother calls from the kitchen. "Emma, are you coming?" After a few minutes, her mother walks out into the garden. "Emma, I've called you twice already," she says. "But I don't want to talk to you, and I don't want to eat anything. Grandma cannot eat anything anymore," Emma says sadly and angrily at the same time. "Emma, Grandma has been dead for a week now. In three days, there is the funeral. You have to slowly calm down." Emma jumps up, "But I don't want to calm down, and I do not want to bury Grandma in the ground!" With these words, she throws her herbal book she has holding in her hands to the floor and runs into the house up to her room. She slams the door shut, throws herself on the bed, and starts to cry. Her mother looks back desperately.

After a while, she goes up to Emma's room and gently knocks on the door. "Emma, do you want to talk?" she asks. "Leave me alone! You do not care that Grandma is dead," cries Emma angrily. Her mother starts to cry, "I do not care, do not care at all," she says softly to herself. Slowly she goes back down to the living room. Her eyes are noticeably red from crying. She looks at the phone. Determined, she reaches for the receiver and begins to dial.

"Hello. Central Hospital Düren. Weniger on the phone."

"Hello, Mister Weniger. This is Misses Neuberger. Would it be possible, please, to speak to Doctor Wegemann?"

"May I ask in what matter do you call?" Mister Weniger wants to know. "My mother died in your hospital last week. She was on Doctor Wegemann's ward," Misses Neuberger answers. "Oh, I'm sorry!" Mister Weniger hesitates for a moment, then he asks, "Are you the mother of little Emma?"

"Yes," replies her mother, "do you know my daughter?" she asks surprised. "Yes, she called here about two weeks ago to talk to Doctor Wegemann." "She has what?" Emma's mother interrupts Mister Weniger. "Oh, you do not know it yet?" apologizes Mister Weniger. "No, she did not tell me," Emma's mother replies in surprise. "Did Doctor Wegemann talk to her?" Emma's mother wants to know. "Yes, she has." Mister Weniger briefly tells the mother what Emma has done to reach the doctor so she can help her grandmother. Touched by the story, her mother starts to cry again. "I have a brave little girl," her mother says softly. "Yes, and the little fighter nature is obviously still on it," replies Mister Weniger. "Thanks," says Emma's mother. "With pleasure. I'm trying to connect you now. All the best for you!" Mister Weniger offers. "Thank you! And for Emma, too!"

"Wegemann. Hello, Misses Neuberger," the doctor greets Emma's mother. "Hello, Doctor Wegemann, please excuse the interruption."

"You don't disturb me. How are you? How is Emma?" the doctor wants to know. "I'm fine with the circumstances, but Emma…she's not feeling well. I feel like it is getting worse every day. She does not want to talk to anyone, she does not want to eat properly, and she cries all day. Sometimes she sits for hours with her herbal book in the garden and just does not do anything," says her mother full of concern. "That doesn't sound good," agrees the doctor. "Do you have any idea how I can help?" Doctor Wegemann asks. "Maybe I have one idea, but I do not know if that's possible," replies Emma's mother. "Tell me. I'll see what I can do," the doctor offers. The mother hesitates for a moment, then she says, "There's the older man Emma made friends with. His name is Alois."

"Yes, that's right," confirms the doctor.

"Anyway, I thought you might be able to contact him to tell him about Emma. Maybe it would help her...and maybe Alois, too?" the mother says hesitantly. The doctor thinks, "I think that might not be a bad idea. The two are in the same situation and may be able to help each other," Dr. Wegemann reasons. "Would you do that for Emma?" the mother asks carefully. "Yes, of course. I'll try it," replies the doctor. "I am infinitely grateful to you, Doctor Wegemann!" "Alright, I like to help if I can!" The doctor and Emma's mother decide that Doctor Wegemann will call Alois to tell him about Emma. The mother asks the doctor to give him her phone number, hoping Alois will get in touch. In fact, Alois answers just 15 minutes later.

"Hello! This is the Neuberger residence!"
"Hello, Misses Neuberger. This is Alois Wiesnhuber."
"Mister Wiesnhuber, it's nice to get in touch,"

says Emma's mother. "Gladly, but please call me Alois," he replies gently. "That's nice of you. My name is Johanna," says Emma's mother. "Pleasant to talk with you," answers Alois. Emma's mother briefly tells Alois what the doctor has already told him. Together, they are considering a plan to help Emma. They want to implement this in three days.

"Emma, please get dressed for the funeral," Emma's mother asks. Reluctantly, Emma walks into her room, stands in front of her bed and looks at her clothes, which her mother has put out for her. She begins to cry again. So today is supposed to be the day her beloved Grandma is buried. Emma goes through the last hours with her grandmother. How they told stories together, how they cried together, and then the farewell. The farewell was final. "Definitely because of the bad stomach cancer," Emma thinks angrily. She is so engrossed in her thoughts that she does not notice how the doorbell rings. Only the knock on her door makes her startle. When she does not answer, a voice familiar to Emma sounds. "Emma, are you in there? It's Alois," says Alois cautiously. Emma opens her eyes, runs to the door, opens it, and hugs Alois. "Alois…what are you doing here?" asks Emma quite surprised. Alois strokes Emma's hair, "Well, it's always good to have a friend by one's side, especially if the friend can help. Maybe I can be your friend who helps you?" asks Alois. Emma nods, "You can be my friend. You're the best friend I have." Emma starts to cry. "And you are the very best little friend that I have," says Alois affectionately. "Besides, I had to see you again. You have offered me to swing on your swing and slide on your slide," Alois tries to cheer Emma. Now Emma has to laugh. "Yes, I have," she replies. Alois looks at Emma, "Are you finished, or do you still have to change your clothes?" he asks softly. "I still have to change my clothes," Emma

85

answers sadly again. "What do you think if you get ready now and I accompany you to the funeral?" Emma looks surprised, "Will you really come with me?" she wants to know. "Of course, we are friends, and friends are always there for each other," says Alois. Emma smiles, goes to her room, and changes her clothes. Afterwards she travels with Alois and her parents to the small chapel, where the funeral is taking place.

It is the first memorial service that Emma experiences. Uncertain, she goes to the little chapel. She holds her mother on her left hand and Alois on her right hand. In the chapel she sees a large altar like she has seen before in church. In front of the altar is a table with a vessel she has never seen before. She would like to know what that is, but she does not dare to ask. Emma, Alois, and Emma's parents sit in the front row. Emma looks at the two wreaths with their beautiful bows. She turns back. People are still coming to the little chapel. "Who are all these people?" Emma wants to know. "These are all people who knew Grandma," replies her mother. "But there are so many," says Emma impressed. Her mother is smiling. Emma hesitates, then she dares to ask, "Mama, what is that vessel on the table?" Emma's mother looks at her daughter, "This is an urn, Emma." The mother hesitates. "And what's in the urn?" Emma asks. The mother swallows. "There is a grandma in there," she answers softly. "Grandma?" asks Emma in amazement. "How does Grandma fit in there?"

"I'll explain that to you after the memorial service, little one," the mother answers softly.

The funeral begins.

Natural burial

Four weeks later, Emma and her mother sit in the Forrest in front of the tree under which Emma's grandmother was buried. "It seems weird that Grandma is lying here under the tree," Emma says softly. The mother nods. "Do you think Grandma is feeling better now?" Emma asks cautiously. "I'm sure she's feeling better now. You know, she does not feel any pain now," her mother tries to explain. "But I still cannot imagine that a human being would simply be burned to fit in an urn," says Emma sadly. "I know, Emma, I think it's a strange idea, too," replies her mother. The mother starts to cry. "Mama, why are you crying? You do not cry otherwise." Emma's mother wipes her cheeks, "But, Emma, I'm crying at other times. I'm just trying to hide it from you," her mother says sadly. "But why? I'm crying in front of you," Emma strokes her mother's arm. "You know, little one, you've been so sad the last few weeks that I just did not want you to be even sadder or worried," replies her mother. Emma looks at the tree, then says, "But mom, if you're sad and do not cry, it's much worse. Besides, I was very angry with you because you were not sad. I always thought you wanted Grandma to die." The mother shakes her head, "No, I certainly did not want that. But I could not do anything about it. I tried to accept it. Nevertheless, it hurt a lot... and it still hurts a lot," her mother says softly. "It hurts me, too," Emma tries to comfort her mother. After a moment's hesitation, Emma looks at her mother, "Do you really think Grandma is back with all the people she would like to see again?" asks Emma. "I do not know, Emma, but I just want to believe it. It's a nice idea that Grandma is not alone now." Emma nods. "Maybe Grandma is watching us now, too?" says Emma and looks up into the sky. "Yes, maybe," agrees her mother and looks up as

90

well. "I miss Grandma very much," her mother says softly. "Me too, Mom. Me, too. But you know, as long as we think of Grandma, she always lives on in our hearts, says Alois." The mother nods, "I'll certainly do that, my little one," says her mother. "I'll always think of her, too," replies Emma. Emma looks at the tree again. "Mom, why was Grandma actually buried here and not in the cemetery where everybody else is?" she asks with interest. "You know, Emma, Grandma never really liked cemeteries. She always said that she does not want to be so confined among all the graves. Besides, she always found the neglected graves to be very bad. She said she never wanted such a grave, but at the same time she did not want to be a burden to anybody. The most important thing was that she loved the forest and the animals so much. She always said that she felt free and safe in the forest at the same time." Emma nods, "Yes, Grandma has always told of the animals in the forest," she agrees with her mother. "Do you know what I like?" Emma asks her mother. The mother shakes her head, "No, what?" "I think it's great that Grandma is here with her animals now. Certainly a few birds or squirrels live in Grandma's tree. Oh, and maybe even hedgehog and deer come over!" Emma laughs, "Not so bad of Grandma to pick such a great place above all. From here you can see the beautiful stars and the moon in the dark." Her mother nods. "You're right," she agrees with a smile to Emma. "Nice here with you, Grandma" sighs Emma.

Together they sit still for a long time in the Forrest in front of the tree under which Emma's grandmother was buried and look into nature, which Grandma so loved.

About the Author and Other Contributors

Daniela Landsberg

Daniela Landsberg, born on February 29, 1980 in Mainz, studied biology, German and psychology. Her first short story came while she was studying to become a teacher when she wanted to show her lecturer that Christmas doesn't always mean "perfect world" and "big family." When she was writing the short story, she found that she enjoyed writing it and decided to continue writing. When she's not writing, she likes to spend time with her cats, try to learn the piano, and get her chocolate addiction under control. As a former tournament dancer, you don't see her addiction. Daniela is an absolute night person, and as a person with Asperger's syndrome, she enjoys the peace and quiet when all other living beings are sleeping.

Dr. Rolf Peter Hampel-Landsberg, MD

Dr. Rolf Peter Hampel-Landsberg, MD, born on May 1, 1962 in Frankfurt am Main, is a specialist in cardiac and thoracic surgery. He never thought that he would illustrate a children's book. After his wife's manuscript had been ready for years and no one was found for the illustrations, she convinced him to just start drawing. What he initially thought was just a funny idea quickly became a reality. He noticed that he enjoyed drawing and painting and that it even balanced out his hectic professional life. From their start to finish, all ten drawings for the children's book were created within a very short time. After tons of drawing and painting utensils were purchased and the joy of painting developed, he and his wife decided that he would continue to illustrate his wife's books for children. In addition to this newly gained hobby, his other hobbies alongside his wife include motorcycling, dancing, playing the piano, playing board games, and watching soccer and Formula 1.